Getting To Know...

Nature's Children

COYOTE

Caroline Greenland

GROLIER
B O O K S

Facts in Brief

Classification of the Coyote

      Class: *Mammalia* (mammals)

      Order: *Carnivora* (meat-eaters)

      Family: *Canidae* (dog family)

      Genus: *Canis*

      Species: *Canis latrans*

World distribution. Exclusive to North and Central America. Found from Panama through western North America, up into Alaska.

Habitat. Plains and lightly wooded areas; have also adapted to forests, bushlands, and tundra.

Distinctive physical characteristics. Bushy tail; large pointed ears; slender muzzle; yellowish-gray fur.

Habits. Mates for life; active mainly at night; sometimes hunts in packs; noted for eerie howl that usually is heard at dusk and dawn, but also at night.

Diet. Mainly small animals; sometimes birds, deer, pronghorns, insects, and vegetation.

Canadian Cataloguing in Publication Data

Greenland, Caroline.
  Coyote

(Getting to know—nature's children)
Includes index.
ISBN 0-7172-1924-0

1. Coyotes—Juvenile literature.
I. Title. II. Series.

QL737.C22G73 1985   j599.74'442   C85-098709-1

Have you ever wondered . . .

what coyotes are famous for?   page 5

if young coyotes like to play?   page 6

how to tell a coyote from a wolf?   page 10

how many kinds of coyotes there are?   page 11

where coyotes like to live?   page 12

what a coyote's coat is like?   page 15

if coyotes come in different colors?   page 15

how coyotes mark their territory?   page 16

if a coyote can see well?   page 18

what a coyote eats?   page 20

when coyotes hunt?   page 20

if coyotes hunt alone?   page 22

what hunting tricks coyotes use?   page 25

why coyotes howl?   page 26

how fast a coyote can run?   page 30

whether coyotes can swim?   page 30

how a coyote finds a mate?   page 33

what a coyote's den is like?   page 34

how many babies a mother coyote has?   page 40

what baby coyotes look like?   page 40

how a mother coyote protects her babies?   page 42

if a father coyote helps look after the cubs?   page 44

when young coyotes leave home?   page 46

Words To Know   page 47

Index   page 48

Yip-yip-yip-awhooo! A yelping howl echoes through the night. One by one more howlers join in until there is a loud chorus of yips and yelps. What could be making all that noise? It is a group of coyotes "singing" to each other. No one knows what they are saying, but whenever two or three coyotes are in the same neighborhood chances are the singing will begin.

Howling is the coyote's trademark, but it isn't the only thing coyotes are famous for. They are known as sly, crafty chicken snatchers and cattle thieves—too fast to be caught but too bad to be ignored.

Do coyotes deserve this bad reputation? Not really. In fact, coyotes' main source of food is small mammals, such as mice and rabbits—the very animals that eat the farmers' crops. In short, coyotes are both friend as well as foe to a farmer. And after all, if they do sometimes prey on livestock, they are just doing what they have to to survive.

Opposite page:
This relative of Rover is most famous for its haunting howl.

Cub Capers

Young coyotes like nothing better than to play. If you could sneak up on some coyote brothers and sisters, here is what you might see.

One young coyote rolls on its back while its brother tugs playfully at an ear. A sister tosses a stick high in the air and tries to catch it. Most of the time she misses and the stick lands on her nose!

Not far away another cub is trying to sneak up on a squirrel. But just when it is about to pounce, the squirrel bounds up a tree and teases the cub with its noisy chatter.

The mother and father are there, nearby, keeping watch over the cubs, ready to shoo them into their den at the first sign of danger.

What lies ahead for these young cubs? What have they learned about hunting, avoiding enemies and howling? Let's find out.

Coyote Cousins

Coyotes belong to the same family as foxes, Timber Wolves and dogs. Can you think of some things these animals have in common?

Well, they all have four fairly long legs and fluffy tails. They also have long, thin snouts and sharp pointed teeth. These teeth are called "canines."

Although the coyote's scientific Latin name, *Canis latrans*, means "barking dog," the coyote is more like its cousin the Timber Wolf than a dog. Indeed, coyotes look so much like Timber Wolves that they are sometimes mistaken for them. Coyotes are sometimes even called "brush wolves."

A coyote has a smaller nose pad, but bigger and pointier ears than a wolf.

Coyote or Wolf?

Imagine that you are walking through the woods one late fall afternoon. Out of the corner of your eye, you see a brownish gray animal bounding out of sight. What was it? A coyote? A wolf? If the animal had stayed a while longer, you might have been able to tell.

One of the big differences between coyotes and wolves is size. Full-grown male coyotes weigh anywhere from 9 to 23 kilograms (20-40 pounds). Wolves can be two to three times larger.

But perhaps the easiest way to tell the two animals apart is by their calls. Wolves give one long sorrowful howl at a time. In contrast, coyotes start with a series of baying yelps, ending in a longer quavering howl.

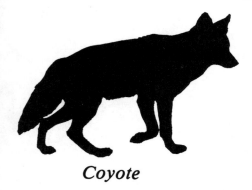

Coyote

Wolf

A Successful Survivor

There are 19 kinds of coyotes in North America. Each kind is slightly different in size or color. But all coyotes have one thing in common: they are very good adapters. In other words, they can change the way they live, including their diets, to make use of what is available.

This gives the coyote an advantage over most animals, who need a certain kind of food or environment to survive. Because the coyote is so good at adapting it has managed to spread across most of North America.

Where coyotes live.

Coyote Country

Coyotes seem to feel at home in all kinds of places. Forests, parklands, grassy meadows and even the tundra provide this adaptable animal with enough cover and food to survive.

Unlike most animals, coyotes even adjusted to living near people! As more and more forested land was cleared by the early settlers for farmland, the number of mice and other rodents increased. To a coyote, these animals are a yummy meal. A field full of rodents is a feast!

Even though coyotes often live near people and benefit from them, they are shy and slightly suspicious of humans. They are also smart enough to stay out of sight. So who knows? If you live in the country, you may even have a family of coyotes hunting and playing and sleeping close by without realizing it.

With its long legs, small feet and muscular body, the coyote is built for speed.

A Warm Coat of Many Colors

Coyotes that live in northern areas where winters are cold grow an extra-thick winter coat. It is made up of two layers. The outer layer of coarse guard hairs helps to shed rain and snow. Under this is a thick warm underfur to trap in body heat.

The coyote's coat has four colors. Can you count them? The coyote has lots of *gray* fur on the main part of its body that gets darker toward its hind end. Its legs, paws, nose and the back of the ears are almost *yellow*, and its throat, stomach and inside the ears are *white*. Take a look at the tip of the tail to see the last color—*black*.

A coyote's coat changes color with the seasons. In order to blend in with the dark summer plants, the coyote has a darker coat in the summer than the winter. Where a coyote lives affects its coat color too. Mountain coyotes that must blend in with the dark shadowy forests tend to be darker than those living in desert areas.

Opposite page:

The coyote can tilt, point and flatten its ears--all the better to hear with.

15

Home Territory

Do you have a special route that you always take to a friend's house? Coyotes use special routes all the time. They have well-worn trails that they follow just as you follow the sidewalks and shortcut paths through your own neighborhood. But coyotes do not use these routes to visit friends. They are *hunting* routes. How far a coyote will travel while hunting depends on the amount of food available. If there is lots of food, the coyote's hunting territory may be small. If food is scarce, it will be larger.

The coyote does not patrol its territory constantly to keep out intruders. Instead it carefully marks the border of its range to warn other coyotes to stay out. To do this it sprays urine and musk on certain trees, fence posts and rock piles. The strong smell of these substances warns other coyotes that the area is already taken and that they should move on.

The coyote can hear a mouse scurrying under a foot of snow.

Super Senses

If you looked a coyote right in the face, the first thing you would notice are its yellow, slightly slanted eyes. They seem to watch your every move. With these crafty-looking, watchful eyes it is no wonder that the coyote is considered sly and cunning.

You might be surprised to learn that the coyote has relatively poor sight and only uses its eyes to detect movement. Fortunately, its senses of hearing and smell make up for its poor vision.

The coyote's wide, pointed ears are constantly at attention, ready to pick up the slightest sound. And the black, quivering nose at the tip of its long, narrow muzzle can pick up a new smell long before you could catch a whiff.

A coyote often goes around with its mouth wide open. In fact, it can stretch its mouth wider than either a dog or a wolf.

Dinner on the Move

A coyote needs a good sense of smell and sharp hearing. Why? Its dinner does not come on a plate like yours does. It must hunt for its food. And the coyote's favorites—rabbits, voles, moles, Ground Squirrels, chipmunks and Woodchucks—all move quickly so it has to be alert and quick too.

The coyote usually hunts at night and stalks its prey as many meat-eaters do. It is as quiet as possible as it pads through the countryside, sniffing here, sniffing there. Once in a while it stops. It listens intently for any small rustle in the grasses. When it hears or smells food . . . pounce!

The black leatherlike nose pad is a protective covering for the coyote's sensitive smelling apparatus.

Share and Share Alike

Sometimes two heads are better than one. Perhaps that is why two coyotes sometimes work together to find food. If the coyote team is stalking a rabbit, one coyote attracts the rabbit's attention while the other sneaks up from behind and takes it by surprise. As many as 10 coyotes have been known to hunt as a pack and stalk a larger animal such as a deer or antelope.

Coyotes are also not above eating an animal that is already dead. To take advantage of this opportunity, the coyotes keep a careful watch on the sky. If they see vultures soaring, they follow the birds to where they land. Chances are that the vultures have swooped down on a dead animal. The coyotes quickly drive the vultures away and take the free meal for themselves.

If this coyote opened its mouth you'd see 42 teeth made for grasping, shredding, tearing and shearing.

Tricks of the Trade

Coyotes do not steal only from vultures. They steal from badgers too. Badgers often scare mice, squirrels and pocket gophers out of their burrows by furiously digging into their holes. The coyote knows that the animal inside will try and get away from the badger. Sure enough, up it pops through an escape hole—and pounce!—the coyote has another meal.

The coyote has even been seen "playing possum" to attract food. Pretending that it is dead, it waits for a crow to come and investigate. Once the crow is close enough, the coyote leaps up and catches the unsuspecting bird.

By using these hunting tricks for catching dinner, the clever coyote rarely goes hungry. If all of its tricks fail and the coyote cannot find enough meat, it will eat a wide variety of plants, including fruit and even acorns.

When food is plentiful, a coyote travels no more than eight kilometres (5 miles) a day.

Night Concerts

Coyotes do not need telephones—they howl their messages around the countryside.

The urge to contact other coyotes can strike anytime during the night, but usually coyotes do most of their howling just as the sun is rising or setting.

If possible, the coyote howls from a hill. Once it is sitting comfortably high, it throws its head back and howls out its mournful yip-yip-yip-awhoooo. If another coyote is in earshot (and do not forget that they have sharp hearing), there is sure to be an answering howl. Soon the two coyotes start howling together, and the coyote concert begins in earnest.

Though coyotes come out most often at night, they can sometimes be seen in the mornings and late afternoons.

No one is sure why coyotes do so much howling. Whatever can they be telling each other night after night? Sometimes they are trying to impress a potential mate. Other times they may be warning intruders off their territory. Or they may be teaching their young their amazing trick of throwing their howl so that it seems to come from a long way off.

Silent Signal

Howling is not the only noise coyotes make. Depending on their mood, they are also good at barking, growling, wailing and even squealing. But coyotes also send silent messages to each other. How?

Like their cousins, the Timber Wolves and foxes, coyotes have a hidden gland at the base of their tails. This gland contains a strong-smelling scent that is slightly different for each animal. By smelling this scent, one coyote can tell if another is a friend . . . or an enemy. It is rather like you recognizing someone by their perfume or cologne even before you turn around to see who is there.

Besides howling, coyotes also growl, hiss, whine and squall.

All-Star Champion

Do not enter a race with a coyote. You will lose. An alarmed coyote can reach a speed of 64 kilometres (40 miles) per hour in seconds flat. The coyote's body is built for speed. It has powerful muscled legs and a slim body. Its dog-like paws have claws that give the coyote a good grip on the ground.

Even more amazing is how quickly a coyote can change directions while running full speed. If a sudden noise attracts its attention or if it detects a strange smell, the nimble-footed coyote turns in mid-stride to investigate. Its long, fluffy tail acts as a rudder in the air and balances the coyote.

The coyote can also swim if necessary. And it is an accomplished jumper. When trying to catch a mouse or grasshopper for a snack, this agile animal can jump more than four metres (12 feet). That would be like you leaping over seven school desks and landing on your feet!

The coyote gets ready for winter early, growing in its thick coat by late September.

Coyote Courtship

Each year, around February, coyotes mate. The same male and female often stay together for years. But if a coyote has never had a mate before or if it has lost its mate, it must try to attract one. How?

Male coyotes do not send valentines or flowers to impress a female. Instead, they compete in howling contests. Whoever howls loudest and longest is almost sure to win the female. Sometimes these howling matches can end up in a fight. The female in question then gets to choose her mate, most likely the winner of the contest. The unsuccessful suitors then start competing all over again for another unattached female while the new couple heads off to start their life together.

Alone for now—but not for long.
February is coyote mating time.

House Hunting

Like all new couples, the coyotes must find a suitable home or den. Choosing a place for a den is up to the female. She carefully scouts their range until she finds a safe and well-hidden location. She will probably return to the same den year after year.

The female seldom goes to the trouble of digging a den from scratch—even though she is an excellent digger. Why waste time and energy if you can find an abandoned marmot or badger burrow? The coyote makes the old burrow her own by adding on some more rooms and corridors until the den is about two to three metres (9 feet) long. This will give her cubs lots of room to romp and wrestle.

As she enlarges the den, the coyote carefully removes any extra dirt and piles it outside the entrance. Later she painstakingly spreads the loose earth into a heap fanning out from the hole.

A coyote looks skinnier in summer than in winter. That's because it has lost its heavy winter coat by late spring.

Spare Homes

Now that the main den is completed, it is time for the female coyote to find a few more dens. These other dens—and the coyote may have up to 12 of them—are used in case of emergencies. Now that is thinking ahead!

Sometimes a coyote mother cannot find an old, unused burrow. Then she will have to make do with a hole at the base of a big old tree or between some giant boulders. Or she may search out a dark dry cave or even prepare a den in a hollow log.

The coyote's guard hairs are about twice as long as the hairs of its undercoat.

Overleaf:
These cubs are probably over one month old. That's the age when they start to explore the world outside the den.

Cuddly Cubs

Before her babies are born in spring or early summer, the female coyote thoroughly housecleans her new home. She wants the den to be spotless for the new arrivals.

Usually five to seven cubs are born, but there is one recorded instance of 19 in a litter! The tiny new coyotes have limp floppy ears and a fuzzy covering of woolly hair. A long black stripe runs down their backs. In fact, you could easily mistake them for newborn puppies complete with pushed-in noses and soft whimpering sounds. As with many animal babies, their eyes are tightly closed. They will not open for as long as two weeks.

For the first month, the cubs live solely on their mother's rich milk. Then they are slowly weaned off milk and onto meat. At first they cannot cope with hunks of solid meat. Their mother feeds them meat that she has already chewed and partly digested so that it is much like baby food. The quickly growing cubs gulp it down in no time, and soon they are ready to handle the real thing.

Keeping Babies Safe

The cubs are now allowed just outside the den entrance. They spend much of the day snoozing or romping around. Their mother is always close by and always alert for danger. If she senses a prowling lynx or wolf or other predator, she gives a special warning yelp. Quickly the obedient cubs head for the safety of the den.

If the predator does not go away, the anxious coyote mother may even fake a limp. Off she stumbles, luring the enemy away from the den. Once she is satisfied that her cubs are safe, she doubles back to the den and leaves the enemy wondering if it had dreamed the whole thing!

Dutiful Dad

When the cubs are two months old, they meet their father for the very first time. Where has he been for these eight weeks? Not far away at all.

In fact, dad has been faithfully prowling outside the den, making sure his brand new family was safe and secure. He has also been in charge of bringing food to the mother coyote. Without his presents of food at the entrance hole, she could not have given them all the care and milk they needed in those early days.

Now both parents will look after the cubs together. Their most important job will be to teach their children how to hunt.

The cubs start with something small . . . a grasshopper, perhaps. They learn the fine art of stalking and pouncing and then move on to bigger game . . . mice and voles! They also learn which animals are dangerous to them and where to find shelter in stormy weather. In short, they learn everything there is to know about staying alive.

The coyote is ever on the alert for its enemies--the black bear, the grizzly bear and the cougar.

On Their Own

By fall the young coyotes are encouraged to leave. Thanks to the careful training by their parents, they are ready to be out on their own. They know all the tricks of the trade, and now they must hunt and howl and woo a mate by themselves.

No doubt they will face many dangers. They must be careful to avoid Timber Wolves and Grizzly Bears because both are large enough to kill the smaller coyote. Cougars, Golden Eagles and lynx are also coyote enemies.

But coyotes are clever and, with a bit of luck, these well-trained "teenagers" will live to be 10 years old. During that time they will raise several coyote families of their own.

Special Words

Burrow   A hole in the ground which an animal digs to use as a home.

Cubs   Young coyotes.

Den   Animal home.

Gland   Part of the coyote's body which makes a special scent.

Guard hairs   Long coarse hairs that make up the outer layer of the coyote's coat.

Mate   To come together to produce young. Either member of an animal pair is also called the other's mate.

Prey   An animal hunted by another animal for food.

Rodent   An animal with teeth that are especially good for gnawing.

Stalk   To follow prey stealthily and quietly.

Territory   Area that an animal or group of animals lives in and often defends from other animals of the same kind.

Tundra   Flat land in the Arctic where no trees grow.

INDEX

adaptability, 11, 15

babies. *See* cubs

coat, 15
communication, 5, 10, 16, 26, 29, 33
cubs, 6, 40, 42, 44

den, 34, 37
description, 8, 10, 15, 18, 30
diet, 5, 12, 20, 22, 25
distribution, 11
  map, 11
dog, 8

ears, 18
enemies, 42, 46
eyes, 18

fall, 46
family, 6, 44
female, 6, 33, 34, 42

getting along, 6, 22, 29, 33
guard hairs, 15

habitat, 11, 12
howling, 5, 10, 26, 33
hunting, 16, 20, 22, 25

jumping, 30

life span, 46
locomotion, 30

male, 6, 10, 33, 44
mating, 26, 33

nose, 18

paws, 30
protection, 12, 16, 26, 29, 42, 44

relatives, 8, 10, 29, 46

scent, 16, 29
senses
  hearing, 18, 20, 26
  sight, 18
  smell, 18, 20
size, 8, 10, 11
  illus. 11
spring, 40
summer, 15, 40
swimming, 30

tail, 29,
teeth, 8
territory, 16
Timber Wolf, 8, 10, 29, 46

winter, 15, 33

Cover Photo: Brian Milne (First Light Associated Photographers)

Photo Credits: Tim Fitzharris (First Light Associated Photographers), pages 4, 19, 23, 35; T.W. Hall (Parks Canada), pages 7, 9; Norman Lightfoot (Eco-Art Productions), page 13; Brian Milne (First Light Associated Photographers), pages 14, 36; William Lowry (Lowry Photo), pages 17, 21; Esther Schmidt (Valan Photos), pages 24, 27; Don McPhee (Lowry Photo), pages 28, 41; Stephen J. Krasemann (Valan Photos), page 31; Frank E. Johnson (Valan Photos), page 32; Ontario Ministry of National Resources, pages 38-39, 43; Dennis W. Schmidt (Valan Photos), page 45.

Getting To Know...

Nature's Children

MONARCH BUTTERFLY

Bill Ivy

GROLIER
BOOKS

Facts in Brief

Classification of the Monarch Butterfly

Class: *Insecta* (insects)
Order: *Lepidoptera* (butterflies)
Family: *Danaidae* (milkweed butterfly family)
Genus: *Danaus*
Species: *Danaus plexippus*

World distribution. North, South, and Central America; Europe; and Australia.

Habitat. Require warm sunny weather and access to the milkweed plant.

Distinctive physical characteristics. Orange wings with black lines and a black border with rows of small white spots.

Habits. Slow deliberate flight; active in daytime; lays eggs on milkweed plant; migrates in large swarms for the winter to southern United States, Mexico, and Central America.

Diet. Nectar of flowers, preferably milkweed blooms.

Canadian Cataloguing in Publication Data

Ivy, Bill, 1953-
  Monarch butterfly

(Getting to know—nature's children)
Includes index.
ISBN 0-7172-1923-2

1. Monarch butterfly—Juvenile literature.
I. Title. II. Series.

QL561.D3I95 1985   j595.78'9   C85-098722-9

Have you ever wondered . . .

if Monarch Butterflies deserve their name?   page 6

where Monarch Butterflies can be found?   page 9

where a Monarch mother lays her eggs?   page 10

how many eggs a Monarch mother lays?   page 10

what a Monarch caterpillar does all day?   page 13

what dangers a caterpillar faces?   page 13

how many sections there are to a caterpillar's body?   page 15

how to tell a caterpillar's head from its tail?   page 17

how many eyes a caterpillar has?   page 17

how a caterpillar prepares for its transformation?   page 21

what a Monarch chrysalis looks like?   page 23

what is the first thing a new butterfly does?   page 28

what a Monarch's wings are like up close?   page 31

if butterflies can taste?   page 32

why a Monarch's eyes are so big?   page 32

if the Monarch keeps growing once it is a butterfly?   page 35

what Monarch Butterflies eat?   page 35

what kind of weather the Monarch likes?   page 36

if a Monarch has any way of defending itself?   page 38

what Monarchs do when the weather turns cold?   page 40

how far a Monarch may travel when it migrates?   page 40

how fast a Monarch flies?   page 43

what Monarchs do all winter?   page 44

if Monarchs live very long?   page 46

Words To Know   page 47

Index   page 48

If you sit quietly by a flower garden on a summer afternoon you may be lucky enough to see a butterfly. It is probably looking in the flowers for food.

There are thousands of different kinds of butterflies in the world. Some are almost as big as dinner plates. Others have brilliant colors. Still others, such as the Swallowtail, even have long "tails."

Butterflies come in a wide variety of shapes, colors and sizes, but they all share one thing. They all go through four stages in their lives. You could say that people go through stages too. We all start life as babies, grow into children, then teenagers and finally adults. But through all of these stages we do not change all that much; we just get bigger.

A butterfly looks *very* different in each stage of its life. It starts out as a tiny egg and hatches into a many-legged caterpillar. Then this caterpillar curls up and is wrapped with a thin covering. When it finally breaks out of this "shell" it is a beautiful flying creature—a butterfly.

The Royal Butterfly

Most people agree that the lion is the King of Beasts. But do you know who is king of the butterfly world? It is the Monarch, of course, as its very name suggests.

And no wonder the Monarch Butterfly is considered the king of butterflies. Although their paper-thin wings are fragile and delicate, some Monarchs fly the length of North America in their short lifetimes.

And long-distance flying is just one chapter in the Monarch's amazing life story. Shall we follow it through the others?

The Monarch, like most butterflies, comes out during the day. A moth, on the other hand, comes out at night.

Milkweed Muncher

If you have milkweed plants near your house, you probably also have Monarch Butterflies. The Monarch depends on the milkweed for food and a place to lay its eggs.

Wherever the milkweed grows, the Monarch soon follows. Long ago, Monarch Butterflies were found only in North, South and Central America, but now they also live in Europe and Australia. No one knows how the Monarch managed to cross the oceans, but we do know that when the milkweed plant spread to new countries so too did the Monarch.

The Monarch mother is careful to lay only one egg per plant so that there will be plenty of food for each caterpillar to grow on.

Small Beginnings

The Monarch Butterfly begins its incredible life as a tiny ridged egg no bigger than the head of a pin. When the female butterfly is ready to lay her eggs she carefully searches for suitable milkweed plants. She seems to know that the caterpillars that will soon hatch from the eggs will need fresh, tender leaves to eat. So she is careful to choose only young, healthy plants.

The mother Monarch lays her eggs one by one on the underside of milkweed leaves. When she is done she will have laid about 400 eggs.

You would have to look very carefully to see a newly laid Monarch egg because its creamy yellow color blends in perfectly with the milkweed leaf. But as the caterpillar grows inside it, the egg changes color. It becomes yellow, then light gray and finally dark gray. Then the shiny black head of the newly formed caterpillar can be seen through the egg shell. Four days to a week after the Monarch egg is laid, the caterpillar chews a hole through the egg and slowly crawls out. A caterpillar is born!

Opposite page:

The Monarch mom carefully glues each egg to the underside of a milkweed leaf.

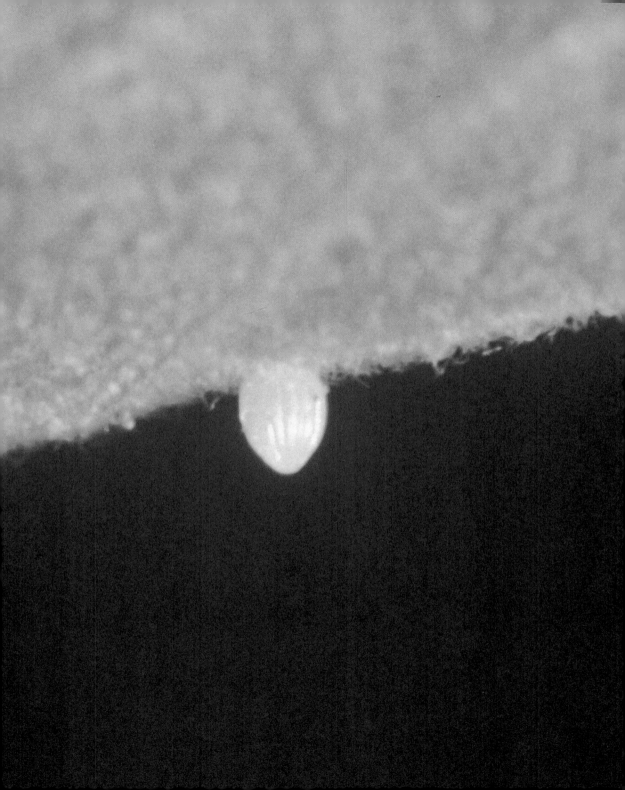

The Eating Machine

Although the newly hatched caterpillar, or "larva," is tiny—only two millimetres (less than one-eighth inch) long—it has an enormous appetite. After dining on its own eggshell, the caterpillar begins to eat the milkweed plant from under its own feet. This miniature eating machine feeds day and night, only briefly stopping to rest between meals. It can eat a whole milkweed leaf in only four minutes. It has very strong jaws and, unlike you, it chews sideways.

During the first day of its life the caterpillar eats its own weight in food. Soon it is twice as big as when it hatched. Yet its life is not one long, happy picnic. It can easily drown in a drop of water, and it has a difficult time protecting itself from hungry birds or other caterpillar-eaters.

Can you imagine eating your own weight in food in a single day? That's what this tiny new Monarch caterpillar is doing, and in about two weeks it will be the size of the full-grown caterpillar you see here with it.

Caterpillar Closeup

After two weeks of almost non-stop eating, the yellow, black and white Monarch caterpillar is about five centimetres (2 inches) long, and it weighs 2700 times more than when it hatched.

Its body is made up of thirteen ring-like sections. Instead of a nose, the caterpillar breathes through holes in these sections. These breathing holes, or "spiracles," look like the portholes along the side of a ship.

On the underside of the caterpillar's body are six small legs and five pairs of large claspers which the caterpillar uses to grip with. It is hard to believe that this worm-like creature will one day become a graceful butterfly.

Yellow, black and white bands make this Monarch caterpillar easy to spot.

Heads or Tails?

You might have trouble telling the caterpillar's head from its tail. Both have long black feelers growing out of them. But if you looked closely you would see that one set of feelers was longer than the other. The longer feelers are on the caterpillar's head.

These head feelers are called "antennae," and the caterpillar uses them to feel its way around. That is important because, although the caterpillar has twelve eyes, they are very small and its eyesight is poor.

Which end is which—can you tell?

Talented Tail

Having a tail that looks like a head is useful to the caterpillar. It confuses birds and other animals that like to eat caterpillars, just as it confused you. To avoid being eaten, the caterpillar wiggles its tail at predators. This protects the caterpillar's head by drawing attention to its tail, where a bite will cause less damage. If that does not work, the Monarch caterpillar may drop off its milkweed plant onto the ground. There it will play dead until the danger has passed. Then the caterpillar will often climb back onto the same milkweed.

The caterpillar's tail feelers are also useful to swish away pesky flies that try to lay their eggs on its back.

The Monarch caterpillar often hangs upside down while enjoying a tasty meal of milkweed.

Preparing for Change

When they are fully grown, Monarch caterpillars eat voraciously. They are preparing for an amazing series of changes that will transform them from slow-moving caterpillars to brightly colored, darting butterflies.

The first signal of the changes to come is that they become very restless. Some leave the milkweed plants that have been their homes since hatching. They wander for as long as two days, looking for a safe place to undergo their amazing transformation. Most choose a spot high off the ground so that they are out of the reach of hungry field mice or other insect-eaters.

Once it has found a safe spot, the caterpillar uses a special gland in its mouth to weave a small silk button underneath a twig or leaf. Turning around, the caterpillar hooks its rear claspers into the silk. Then it swings free, to hang upside down in the shape of the letter "J." What will happen next?

The Little Green House

The caterpillar begins to move. First it arches its back, forcing the skin to split open. Then it wriggles for up to five hours to shed its coat for the last time. When its old skin is gone it looks like a large green water droplet. It has entered its pupa stage.

Slowly this thick, green drop begins to change shape and color. Its outer layer hardens into an elegant emerald case, decorated with gold. This is known as a chrysalis, which comes from the Greek word for golden. The Monarch's little green house with the single ring of golden dots around it hangs perfectly still, but inside something amazing is happening.

This Monarch caterpillar shed its skin four times while it was growing. Now it is shedding for the fifth and final time. It is ending its life as a caterpillar and entering the pupa stage.

Monarch Magic

Inside the chrysalis one of the great wonders of life is taking place. No one fully understands just how this miraculous change happens, but from the soft green liquid inside the chrysalis an adult butterfly will be formed.

For the next nine to fifteen days all is still. Then almost magically, the chrysalis shell turns a rich teal blue and gradually becomes totally transparent. The adult monarch is now visible, its miniature flame-colored wings and jet black body cramped inside. Hanging head down it waits for the right moment to break out of its jeweled cage.

It's hard to believe that inside these two "little green houses" caterpillars are getting ready to become butterflies.

A Brand New Butterfly

The Monarch Butterfly instinctively knows just the right moment to emerge from the chrysalis. It will not come out on a rainy or cool day because it must be warm to be active.

Usually the Monarch emerges on a bright sunny morning. The colorful case stirs and a tiny slit appears on the bottom of it. The chrysalis continues to rip open, and within two minutes a rumpled form tumbles out in a backward somersault and clings to the empty chrysalis.

A butterfly is born!

Taking Wing

The new butterfly has limp, crumpled wings that look like folded parachutes. Immediately, they begin to unfold as the butterfly pumps them full of body fluid from its swollen body. It takes 20 minutes before its wings are full size.

Slowly the Monarch begins to sway back and forth and joins the two halves of its tongue together to form a tube. This is very important for it is this tube that enables it to eat. Next the Monarch rests, waiting for the warmth of the sun to dry and harden its wings. Then, for the first time in its life, this royal butterfly rises up on delicate wings and flies.

It takes a few hours for the butterfly's wings to harden. Until that happens, the butterfly cannot fly.

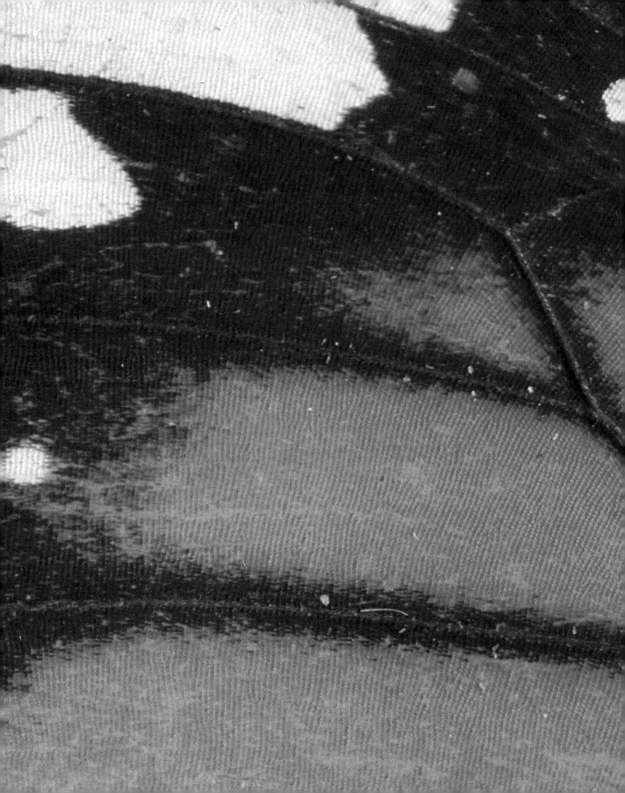

Meet the Monarch

The Monarch has two pairs of vividly patterned wings, covered with millions of tiny, colored scales. These overlap each other like shingles on a roof.

If you were to touch the Monarch's wings these dainty flakes would rub off like fine powder onto your fingers. This is why the family name for butterflies and their relatives, the moths, is "Lepidoptera," a Greek word meaning scale-winged.

Like all insects, the Monarch has six legs and three body sections: the head, thorax and abdomen. But for some reason this butterfly does not seem to need all its six legs. It always holds the front pair folded up close to its body.

The bright colors on the wings are really layers of scales. Underneath the scales the wings themselves are transparent.

Monarch Senses

It is hard to imagine using the soles of your feet for tasting foods but that is what a Monarch does. And a Monarch's feet are much more sensitive to sweetness than your tongue is.

Stranger still are the Monarch's bulging eyes. They seem much too big for its head. It is no wonder they are so big; each large eye contains 6000 lenses! No one is sure how the world looks to a Monarch, but we know that it can detect movement better than almost any other living creature. Just try to catch one!

Despite its superb eyesight, this surprising butterfly relies even more on its sense of smell. Two antennae attached to its head act as the Monarch's nose and ears. They are very sensitive and help direct the Monarch to its favorite flowers.

This Monarch, like most butterflies, has knobs on the ends of its antennae.

Flower Food

In less than a month the Monarch has gone through four stages of life: egg, caterpillar, pupa and adult butterfly. No more changes will take place, nor will the Monarch Butterfly grow. But even though it has stopped growing it still needs energy, so it must eat.

For its first three days as a butterfly the Monarch feeds constantly. Instead of eating leaves as it did as a caterpillar it lives on the nectar of flowers—the same sweet fluid bees use to make honey. The Monarch flits from flower to flower using its hollow tongue to drink the nectar which has formed in the blossom of the flower. When not in use, this handy built-in straw is coiled under the butterfly's head.

Stamp, stamp, yum. Like all butterflies, the Monarch tastes with its feet.

A Happy Wanderer

After feasting for three days, the Monarch butterfly drifts aimlessly over fields and meadows. It may travel great distances in its wanderings, sleeping in any handy tree or bush at night, pausing at any handy flower for a meal when it gets hungry.

Although the Monarch needs the warmth of the sun and loves bright sunny weather, it is often seen flying just before a thunderstorm. For this reason it has been nicknamed the storm butterfly.

When the milkweed is in bloom, Monarchs will choose its flowers over all others. But if there are none around, any flower will do just fine.

Predators Beware!

The Monarch can fly out of the way of ground-dwelling predators such as shrews and mice, and it has come up with an unusual way of defending itself against fast-flying birds. It has a bitter taste that can be poisonous to a bird if it swallows too much butterfly. The Monarch tastes this way because of chemicals in the milkweed plant which it ate as a caterpillar. Birds soon learn that orange and black butterflies are not good food and avoid them.

Another kind of butterfly, the Viceroy, makes good use of the Monarch's bird-proof taste. It looks so much like a Monarch that birds leave it alone as well, even though they would probably find the Viceroy a tasty snack. The Viceroy's Monarch "disguise" is a very effective way of protecting it from hungry birds.

Even though they are look-alikes, there is one way to tell a Viceroy butterfly from a Monarch butterfly. Look at their hind wings. The Viceroy has a black line across its hind wings that the Monarch does not have.

Incredible Journey

Monarchs are the only insects that fly south for the winter. They start out alone as soon as the winds of autumn turn cold, but they may gather in large groups as they wait for good conditions at difficult crossing points. Many will travel almost 3200 kilometres (2000 miles) before they reach their final destination.

The red leaves of autumn tell us this Monarch will soon be gone.

The Monarchs travel by day at about the same speed as a fast jogger, occasionally stopping to feed. Just one "tankful" of nectar can keep them going for a week or more. With good winds pushing them some have been known to travel 130 kilometres (80 miles) in a single day.

The Monarchs follow the same routes and land in the same trees that generations of Monarchs have before them. That is amazing because many of these butterflies have never made the trip before. How they do this is one of the mysteries of the astonishing Monarch.

Winter in the South

Try to imagine so many Monarch Butterflies that you cannot see the bark of the trees that they are roosting on. You cannot see any leaves or pine needles either—just Monarchs, Monarchs, everywhere! Some of these "butterfly trees" become so heavily laden with Monarchs that their branches may actually snap under the weight!

Monarchs from western North America congregate in California along the Pacific coast. Monarchs from eastern North America head for Mexico. One of the most famous of the Monarch's winter "resorts" is Pacific Grove, California. Each year the school children in that area hold a parade to celebrate the Monarchs' arrival.

All winter long, the Monarchs rarely leave their "butterfly trees" except to feed. With the arrival of spring, they are ready to wing their way northward again.

Northward Bound

Many of the Monarchs mate before leaving their winter resting place or on the journey home. They do not stay together after they mate. Instead alone or in small groups they slowly head north. Along the way some of the females stop to lay their eggs. In four to six weeks these eggs will hatch into caterpillars and be transformed into butterflies. By instinct the new butterflies know that they must continue north. And by instinct they know when they have reached their summer homes.

Not all of the butterflies that start the journey finish it. Few Monarchs live to be one year old, and many die on the long hard flights. But there are always new butterflies hatching to take their place in the great northward migration.

Special Words

Caterpillar   The second stage in a Monarch's life. Also called the *larva*.

Chrysalis   The hard case that covers the pupa.

Claspers   The grasping hooks that a caterpillar uses to hold onto a leaf.

Gland   A part of the body where certain substances are made.

Larva   The caterpillar stage of a butterfly or moth's life.

Lens   One part of an insect's eye which helps it to see objects.

Life cycle   The stages in an animal's life from birth to death.

Mate   To come together to produce young.

Migration   A journey that many animals and the Monarch Butterfly make in search of food.

Nectar   The sweet liquid produced by plants which some insects drink.

Pupa   The stage in a butterfly or moth's life before it turns into an adult.

INDEX

adult butterfly, 5-10, 16, 25-47
  antennae, 32
  description, 6, 21, 25, 28, 31, 32, 38
  diet, 5, 9, 35
  distribution, 9, 44
  ears. *See* antennae
  enemies, 38
  eyes, 32
  fall, 40
  feeding, 9, 32, 35, 43
  feet, 32
  female, 10, 46
  getting along, 40, 46
  habitat, 26, 36
  home, 44
  life span, 46
  locomotion, 6, 25, 35
  mating, 46
  migration, 6, 40, 43, 44, 46
  nose. *See* antennae
  protection, 38
  senses, 32
  spring, 44
  summer, 5, 46
  tongue, 28, 35
  wings, 6, 25, 31
  winter, 40, 44, 46

caterpillar, 5, 10-23, 35, 38
  antennae, 17, 18
  change to chrysalis, 23, 25
  description, 5, 13, 15, 17, 21
  diet, 10, 13, 38
  enemies, 13, 18
  feeding, 13, 15, 21
  growing up, 10, 13
  head. *See* antennae
  locomotion, 10, 15, 23
  nose. *See* spiracles
  protection, 18
  sense of sight, 17
  sense of touch, 17
  silk button, 21
  spiracles, 15
  tail. *See* antennae

egg, 5, 10, 35, 46
  description, 10
  hatching, 5, 10, 46
  home, 10
  protection, 10

larva. *See* caterpillar

pupa, 5, 23-26, 35
  change, 23, 25
  chrysalis, 23, 25
  coming out, 26
  description, 23, 25

relatives, 31

stages of life, 5, 35

Cover Photo: K. Janosi (Valan Photos)

Photo Credits: Bill Ivy, pages 4, 8, 11, 12, 18, 19, 20, 22, 24, 27, 29, 30, 33, 37, 39, 41, 42; Norman Lightfoot (Eco-Art Productions), pages 7, 14; Herman H. Giethoorn (Valan Photos), page 34; T.W. Hall (Parks Canada), page 45.